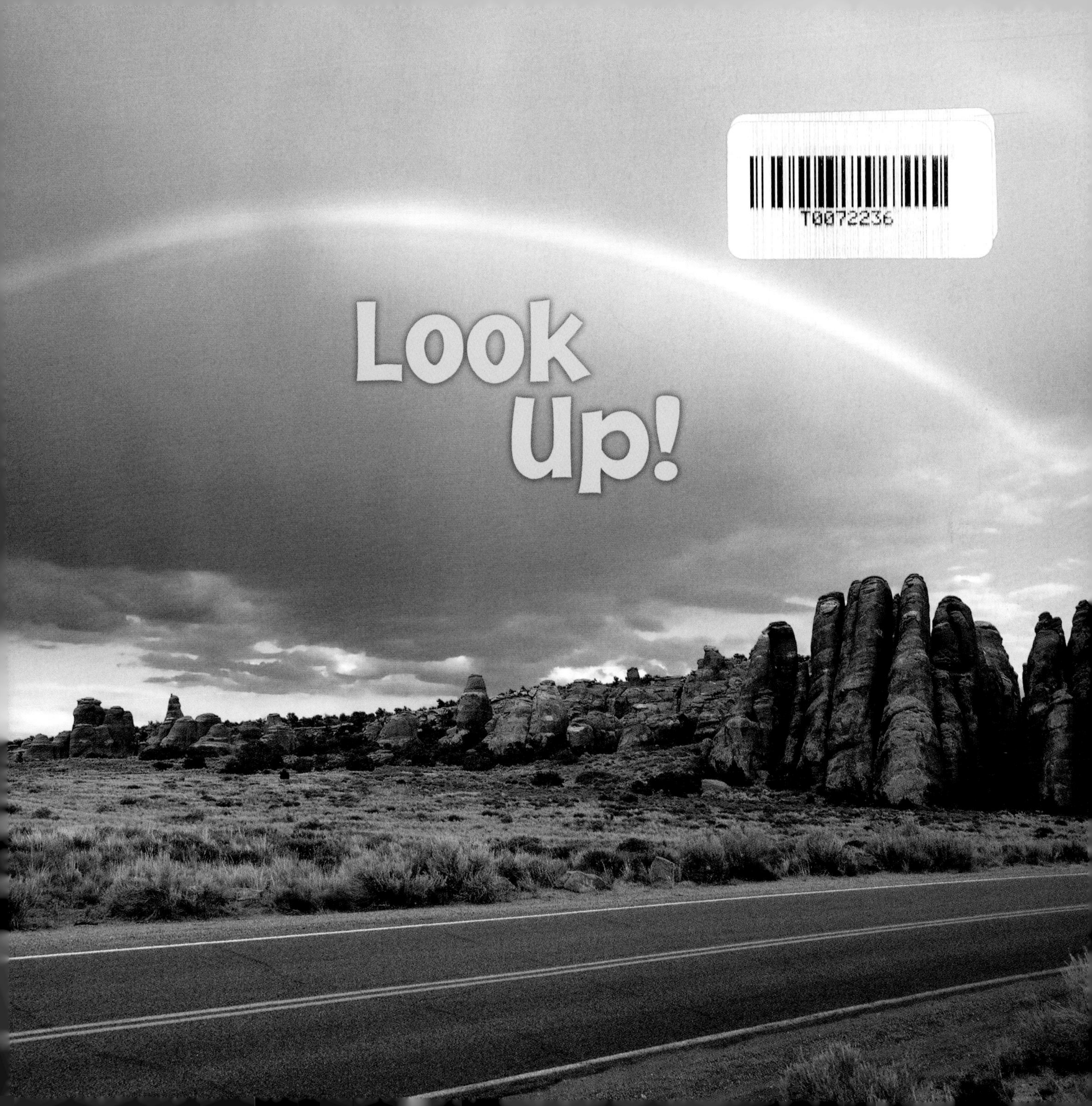
Look
Up!

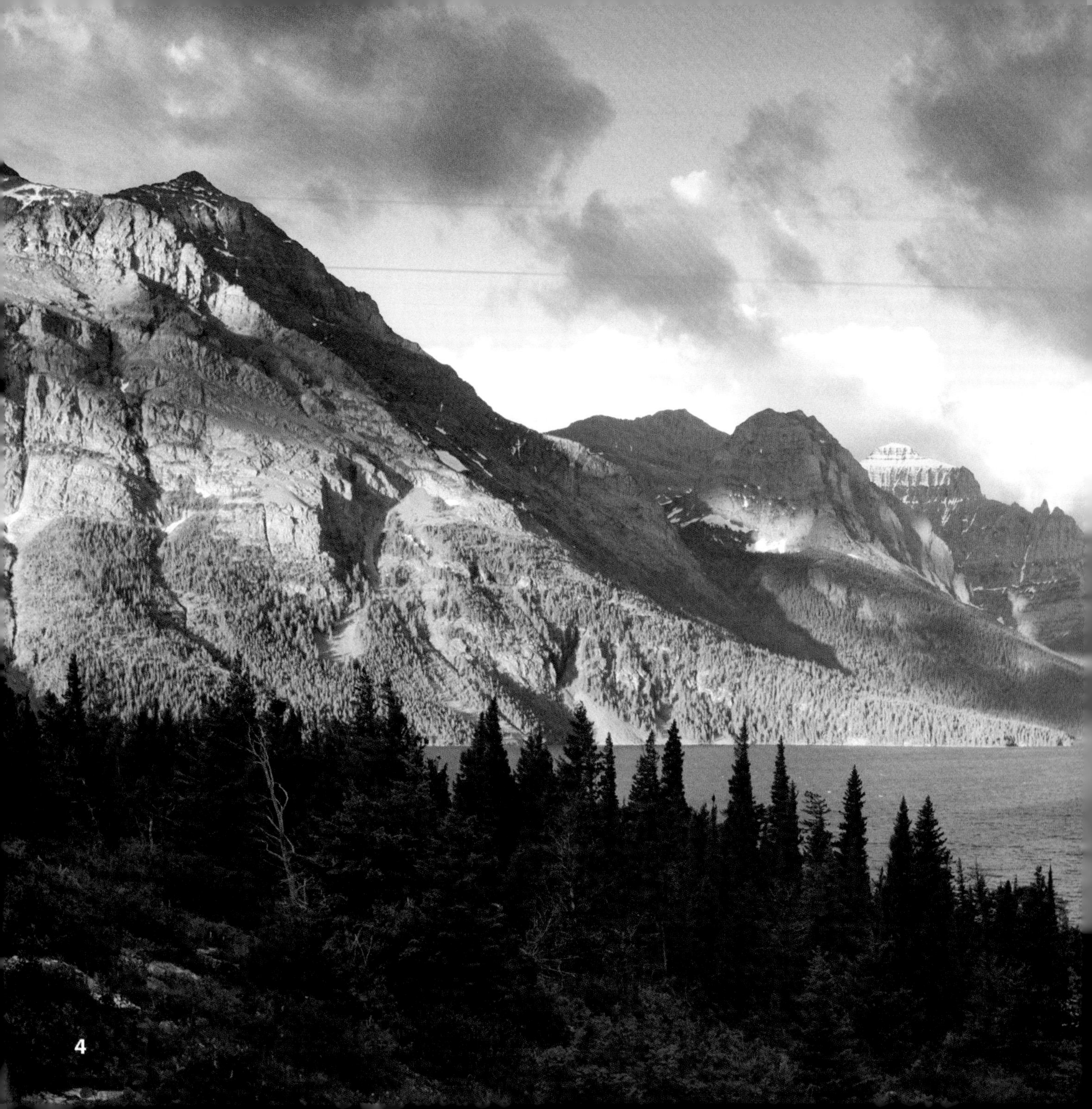

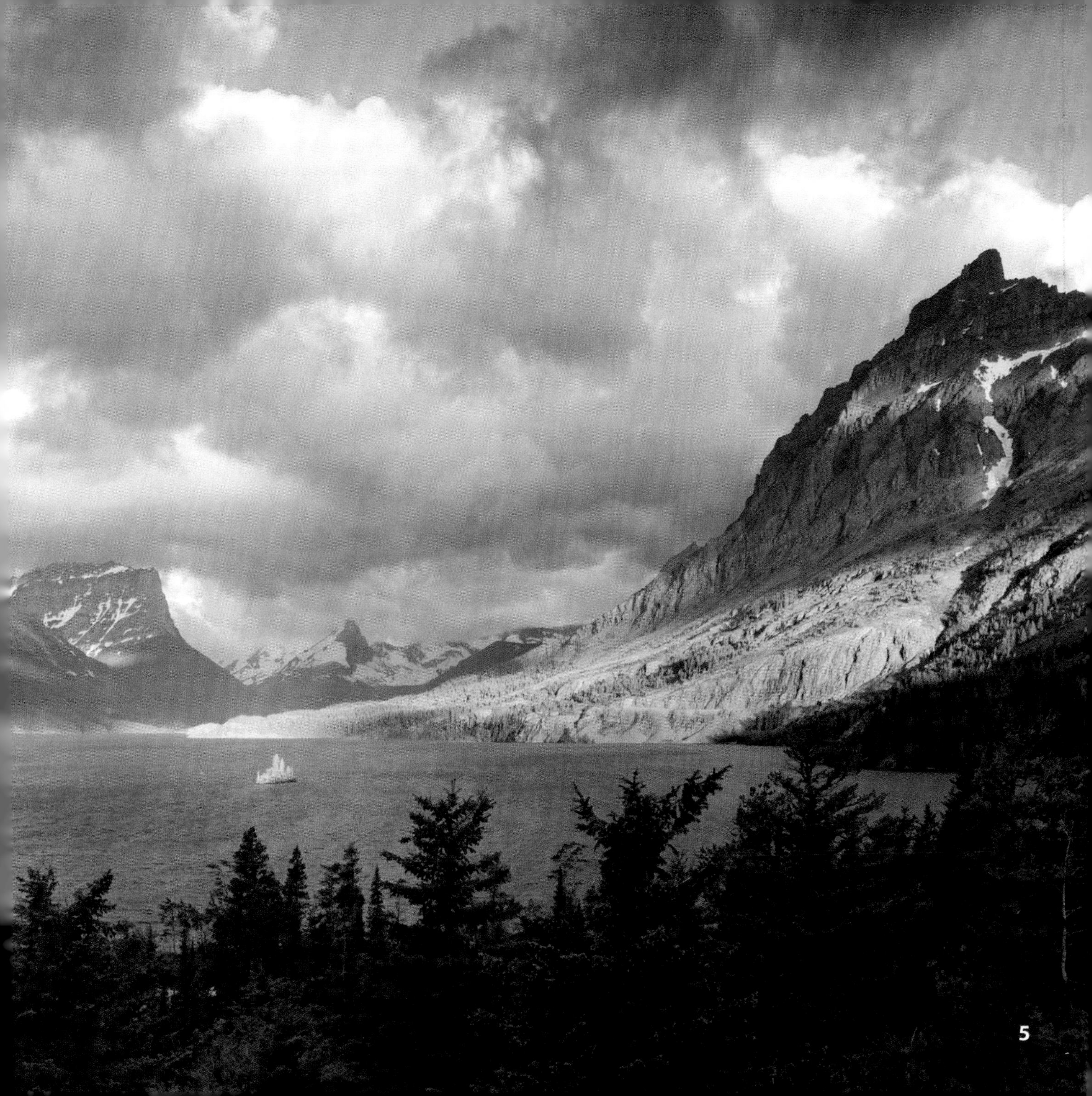

6

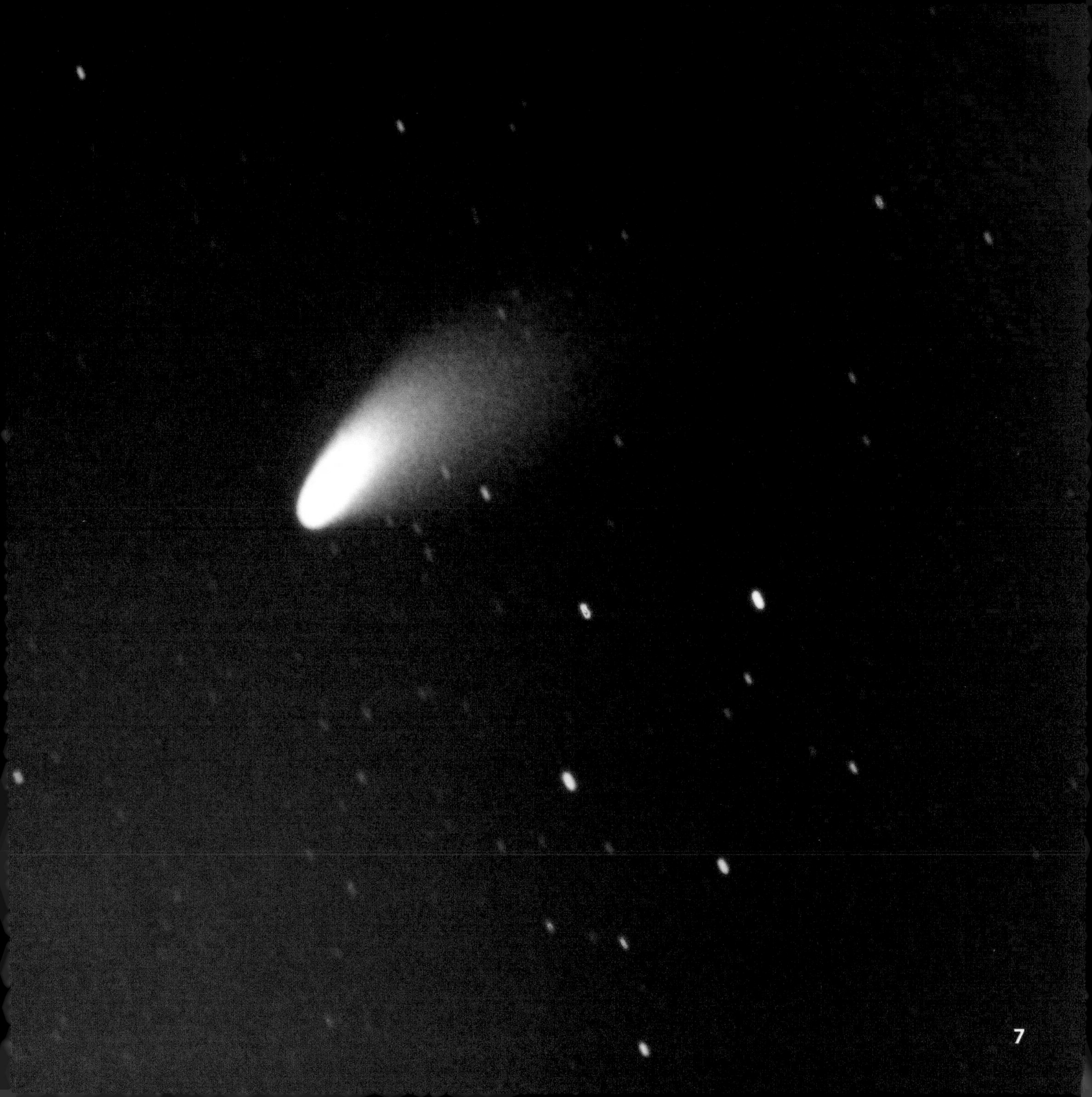

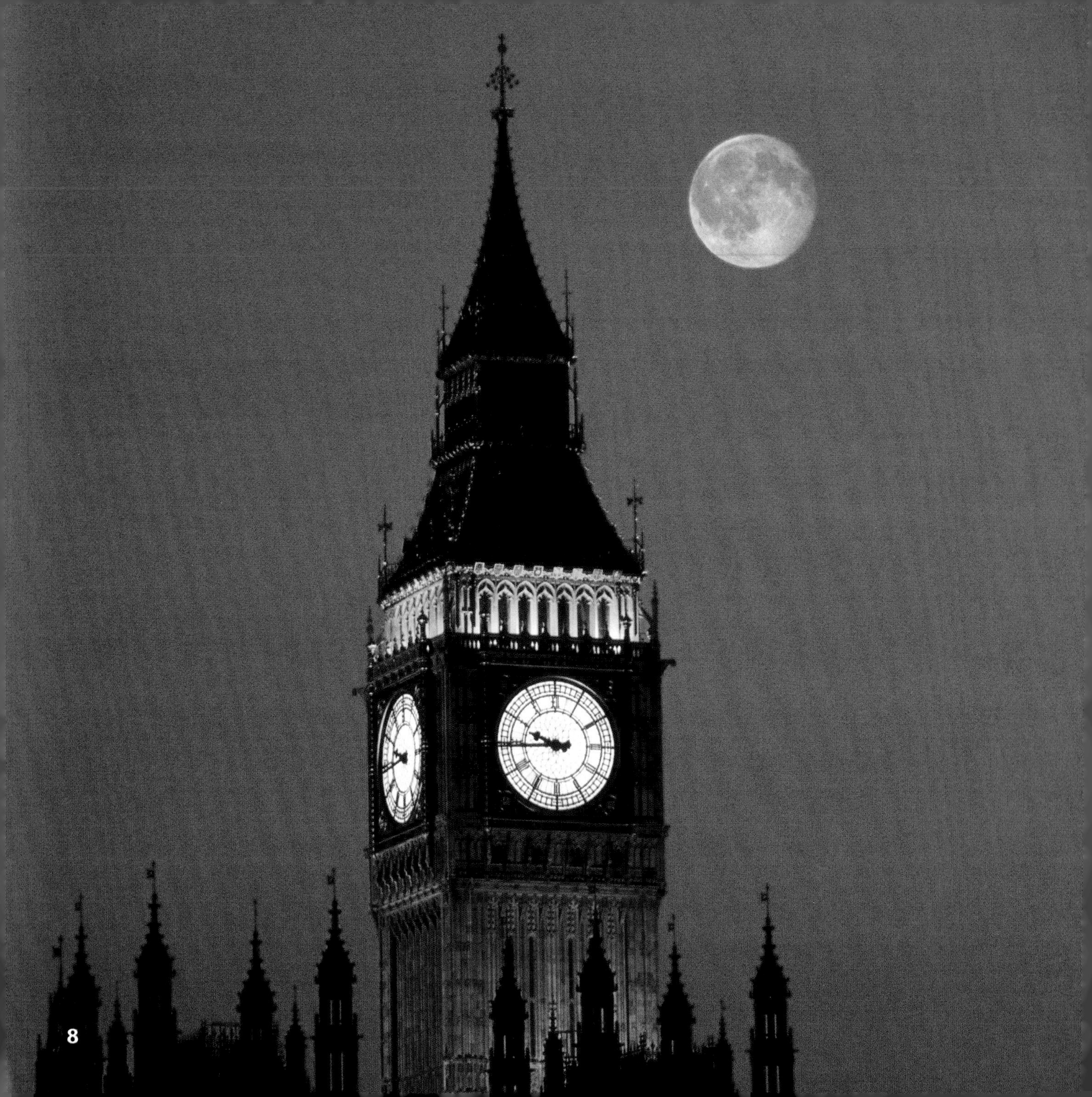